STEPS TO LIBERATION:
THE BUDDHA'S EIGHT FOLD PATH

Steps to Liberation: The Buddha's Eightfold Path

GIL FRONSDAL

TRANQUIL BOOKS

CONTENTS

1
How to Use This Book

Just as in the great ocean there is but one taste—the taste of salt,

so in this teaching and discipline there is but one taste—the taste of liberation.

—*The Buddha (Udana V 5)*

Buddhism is found in just one place—in the people who engage in the practices the Buddha taught. Reading about Buddhism without practicing is like reading a recipe but never cooking the meal. While it may be interesting and educational to read about Buddhist practice, you won't experience the taste of liberation without practicing.

This book is meant to be a practical introduction to the Buddha's most useful and accessible recipe for walking the path to liberation—the Eightfold Path. To support a personal engagement with each of the eight path factors, the book includes reflections and exercises for each factor. Taking the time to do these reflections and exercises is a way to deepen your connection with the Eightfold Path and to better apply it to your life.

It's my hope that the offerings in this book will encourage you to engage in the process of active reflection and contemplation of Buddhist teachings and your relationship to those teachings. There are a number of ways you might do this. You might think about where and when the teachings can be useful in your life. In exploring your relationship to the teachings and practices you might consider how well you understand them, how much enthusiasm you have for them, and the challenges and reservations you have about them. You might come up with questions that bring new perspectives on the teachings.

The value of this book as a basis of reflection on the teachings and their application to your life can be enhanced by reading it slowly, stopping regularly to consider what you have read. It can be useful to only read a few pages each day, perhaps rereading a section a few times throughout the day. Reading slowly and repeatedly will give you time to think about the implications of the teachings, perhaps with each reading thinking of new applications and relevance in your life.

The Eightfold Path is a tremendous support for meditation practice. Practicing the path factors in daily life creates a supportive state of mind for engaging in meditation. Some of the factors are directly applicable to meditation practice. Reflecting on their connection to meditation and how to have them support ones meditation is a valuable exercise. As you read this book you might regularly consider how what you learn can be applied to meditation.

It can be very helpful to discuss your reflections with others. Having conversations about the teachings, the practices, and your findings is one way to develop new understandings about them. Sometimes expressing your ideas out loud provides an opportunity to develop your understanding further. Hearing others discuss their understanding and application of the teachings can open new perspectives and provide inspiration.

It can also be useful to have a "practice journal" in which you write down notes about your experiences practicing with each factor of the Eightfold Path. Sometimes by keeping a journal and rereading your entries, you can better discover how your practice changes and develops over time. It may be possible to notice patterns in how you engage in the practice—for example, you might notice the most common perspectives and concerns you have, or, perhaps, what you tend to ignore or leave out.

One of the ways to read this book and to explore each of the factors of the Eightfold Path is to spend one month studying and practicing each factor. Included in the book are four sets of reflections and practices for each path factor. I recommend spending one week doing each set of exercises before moving on to the next path factor.

Also, during each month try to read or listen to what a variety of Buddhist teachers have said about the factor you're studying. In addition to this book, you might also read Bhikkhu Bodhi's *The Noble Eightfold Path* and Bhante Gunaratana's *Eight Mindful Steps to Happiness*. You can also listen to the talks I've given on the Eightfold Path factors, available on <u>audiodharma.org</u> under Series Talks.

Having the Eightfold Path mature within you is one of the great joys of Buddhist practice. It brings confidence, strength, ease, freedom, and so much more. I hope this little book helps you along the path.

2

The Buddha's Eightfold Path

"It is as if a person, traveling in the forest, were to see an ancient path, an ancient road, traveled by people of former times. Following it, the person would see an ancient city, an ancient capital inhabited by people of former times, complete with parks, groves, and ponds, walled, delightful. Then going to the ruler of the country, the person would say, 'Your majesty, while traveling in the forest I saw an ancient path; I followed it and found an ancient city, an ancient, abandoned capital. Your majesty, restore that city!'

"In the same way I saw an ancient path, an ancient road, traveled by the Awakened Ones of former times. And what is that ancient path, that ancient road, traveled by the Awakened Ones of former times? It is the noble eightfold path: right view, right aspiration, right speech, right action, right livelihood, right effort, right mindfulness, right concentration. That is the ancient path, the ancient road leading to direct knowledge."

—*The Buddha (Connected Discourses 12.65)*

The Buddha's teachings describe an accessible path to liberation. The ancient Buddhist metaphor of a path draws on the idea of a cleared passageway that allows one to move through an otherwise impassable forest. Just as we bring our entire body along when walking on a path in the forest, so a practitioner enters the Buddhist path by engaging all aspects of who he or she is. Yet there's an important difference between a physical path and the one described in the Buddhist literature. A physical path exists whether we walk on it or not. But the Buddhist path exists only in our engagement with it. We create the path with the activities of our minds, hearts, and bodies. All teachings about the Eightfold path are simply instruction indicating how we create the path as we go.

In the version of this metaphor quoted at the beginning of this chapter, the Buddha likens spiritual liberation to a long forgotten, overgrown city deep in the forest. Just as it is possible to reclaim and then inhabit this city once the path to it is found, it is possible to live a liberated life when we have found and walked the path that will lead us to it.

Building on this metaphor of a forest path, the forest's dense undergrowth is like the many mental and emotional obstacles that limit our freedom. As human beings we have our own inner wilderness with its dangers and challenges, but we also have within us what it takes to be free of these dangers.

Because both the path and the obstacles to our freedom are found inside us, the Buddhist path requires us to take responsibility for our thoughts, attitudes, and actions.

It builds on the principle that we can move towards liberation by disengaging from perspectives and behaviors that weigh us down, and replacing them with behaviors that lighten us and support us as we proceed.

The Buddhist path to liberation—known as the Eightfold Path—is made up of eight interrelated practices. The ancient Indian names for these practices are each prefaced by *samma*, a Buddhist word usually translated as "right" or "wise", but which can also mean "proper," "complete," and "in harmony." When "right" is used as the translation, it's useful to think of it as meaning "appropriate," as when we speak of having the "right" tool for a particular task. Because the path is made up of practices rather than beliefs, "right" does not refer to truths that we're obligated to adopt. It also does not involve moralistic judgments of right and wrong. I prefer to think of *samma* as meaning "helpful". The eight "right" practices of the Eightfold Path are perspectives and practices that help us attain the inner liberation Buddhism teaches as real possibilities for each of us.

The first step on the Eightfold Path is Right View, a pragmatic perspective that guides us to the path itself. We can make an analogy with hiking. Hikers in uncharted wilderness must pay careful attention to specific details of their surroundings in order to find their way. They may first have some idea where they're going so they don't wander aimlessly and end up lost. But even when the destination is clear, taking the most direct route may not be possible if it entails plunging into the densest, overgrown parts of the forest or over the steepest cliffs. By knowing what to pay attention to, a hiker can "read" the wilderness and discover clues for what is the best way forward. Similarly, the eight factors of the Eightfold Path are both the clues for finding the path out of the wilderness of suffering as well as the path itself. It is a path to liberation.

For the Buddhist path, the fundamental orienting perspective—called "Right View"—is being guided by the perspective known as the Four Noble Truths. Rather than getting caught up in opinions and abstract interpretations about what we're experiencing, in this approach we learn to first recognize any stress, discomfort, or suffering resulting from how we're relating to what's happening or not happening (the first Noble Truth). We then orient ourselves to notice our contribution to this suffering by discovering the ways we are caught in cravings and clinging (the second Noble Truth). Then we keep our sights and confidence on the possibility of bringing clinging and its resulting suffering to an end (the third Noble Truth).

The final guidepost provided by the Four Noble Truths is the Eightfold Path (the fourth Noble Truth). The Eightfold path is the easiest and clearest road to this liberation from suffering.

Right View is not meant to be the only perspective with which to view our life. Other perspectives are necessary for other purposes. For example, understanding cultural diversity provides important viewpoints for living in a diverse society. Knowing what is expected at work is an important perspective to keep in mind. Taking into account the developmental stages of children is important for parents.

In order to walk the Buddhist path to freedom, Right View is an essential ingredient. It is the perspective needed to find the path in the first place. It points us to what we are doing when we suffer and to how to stop doing this. Part of the value of this perspective is its pragmatic simplicity. It does not rely on any supernatural or mystical beliefs. We are not asked to believe or depend on something we can't know directly for our self, in our self.

The remaining practices of the Eightfold Path are Right Intention, Right Speech, Right Action, Right Livelihood, Right Effort, Right Mindfulness, and Right Concentration. These seven have a mutually supportive relationship with Right View. On the one hand, Right View helps us distinguish between the intentions, speech, ethical actions, livelihoods, and mental efforts that cause suffering and the ones that alleviate it. On the other hand, as we practice the other factors of the Eightfold Path, it becomes easier and more effective to practice Right View: the more the path is cleared, the easier it is to find it.

The potential for practicing the Eightfold Path lies within us. When we practice the factors well, they transform us. They have the ability to reduce and even end our clinging, attachment, fear, hatred, and delusion. When this is done thoroughly, the Eightfold Path is not something we make effort to do. When we are free, there is nowhere we have to go to find freedom. Amazingly, when we live with this freedom, the Eightfold factors are no longer practices; they become the natural expression of liberation. The Eightfold Path becomes who we are.

3

A Life of Mutual Benefit

"A wise person is motivated to benefit one self, others, and both self and others."

—*The Buddha*

Some people live their lives focused primarily on benefiting themselves and those they feel closest to. Others are devoted to benefiting others, sometimes at the expense of themselves. For the Buddha, a wise person is someone who wishes for the good of everyone, oneself included. Our lives are so interconnected that it is not possible to truly benefit oneself while harming others; intentionally harming others always takes a toll on the heart of the person who harms. And we can't be of much benefit to others if we neglect ourselves. The Buddhist path of liberation doesn't neglect either the self or others; it's a path that lies at the intersection of our self and the world.

The Eightfold Path balances caring for our self and others. Each path practice clearly benefits us when we practice them. They help us attain greater ease, integrity, wisdom, and freedom. At the same time, four of the path factors are practices that also bring benefit to other people. For instance, included in the second factor, Right Intention, is to live motivated by goodwill and compassion for others. The next three factors, Right Speech, Right Action, and Right Livelihood, are all concerned with being in the world in such a way that our speech, actions, and livelihood have a helpful, useful, positive impact on others.

In the practice of Right Speech the Buddha encouraged people to speak in ways that are truthful, reliable and trustworthy, choosing speech that "reunites those who are divided, promotes friendship, and speaks words that promote concord." He also encouraged speaking about what is good and beneficial.

Right Action is defined as not killing, not taking what is not given, and not engaging in sexual misconduct. While doing these three things alone provides others with the gift of safety, the Buddha went further by saying that in living a life that doesn't cause harm, practitioners should "abide compassionate to all living beings."

For many people it's through their livelihood that they have the greatest impact on the wider world. The practice of Right Livelihood encourages us to be thoroughly ethical in our work and in life pursuits. Exploiting or harming others through our work is antithetical to Right Livelihood.

While Right Intention, Right Speech, Right Action, and Right Livelihood are practices that have a positive impact on others, we ourselves also benefit when we practice them. One of the great sources of well-being and peace is a clean conscience. Our own ethical integrity can become a meaningful refuge for us.

The last three factors of the Eightfold Path—Right Effort, Right Mindfulness, and Right Concentration—are usually understood as emphasizing care for oneself. All three factors focus on improving the quality of our minds and hearts. Right Effort involves learning to do those things that increase our wholesome states of mind. Right Mindfulness gives us the presence of mind to differentiate between what is wholesome and unwholesome. Right Concentration brings calm, ease, and peace.

The personal benefits that come from the last three factors of the Eightfold Path can also benefit others, because personal well-being is the wellspring for caring for others. As mindfulness and concentration help us be more settled and happy, we have increased motivation to care about others. With increased mindfulness and concentration come increased empathy and appreciation of others.

Some people, however, may feel that any emphasis on benefiting our self is selfish. This could be the case if the effort of self-benefit is a myopic concern for one's own desires at the exclusion of others. However, such selfishness harms the person who is selfish. If we understand what brings and supports personal well-being, we will avoid being selfish. Furthermore, we will not pursue our own well-being at the expense of others.

In Buddhism, benefiting ourselves does not equate to acquiring pleasure, status, or wealth. It entails developing beautiful and wholesome qualities of heart. It is cultivating the kind of inner goodness and peace that help make *how we are* in the world as helpful for others as *what we do*.

For similar reasons, we would not want to engage in activities that benefit others if doing so proved harmful to ourselves in any significant way. How can we really touch the heart of others if our own heart is not well taken care of?

A person focused on mutual benefit does not view life as a competition that only some people can win. Rather, in this approach one considers what is best for the greater good, what the Buddha referred to in the quote above as benefiting "both self and others." This is not a greater good that sacrifices the welfare of some for the welfare of the majority. This greater good is inclusive, using creative thinking that looks for ways to improve the lives of all.

Even though we might speak of certain factors as having particular benefit for oneself, on a deep level there is little distinction between caring for ourselves and caring for others. When we benefit others we're helped in return, not least because our actions strengthen wholesome qualities in ourselves. When we benefit ourselves through developing our integrity, our hearts, and our wisdom, we will inevitably have a positive impact on the people we come in contact with. Conversely, if we intentionally cause harm to others, we will sooner or later discover how this behavior also harms ourselves because of the pain that comes with such intentions. Also, others might retaliate. And over time, no one can escape his or her own conscience.

In practice, a life of mutual benefit does not mean that everything we do has to benefit everyone. If we think of it like that, we can tie ourselves in knots, feeling so overwhelmed we may either do nothing or do too much to be effective. The concept of mutual benefit means that when we care for ourselves in healthy ways we can be reassured that this is for the greater good. When we care for others in healthy ways, it benefits us as well. At different times, in different situations, as we act on different ends of the self/other spectrum, if we see these actions through the perspective or practices of the Eightfold Path, we are working for the greater good of all.

At times it is appropriate, and even important, to

focus on caring for our self. Meditating every morning may be immensely helpful for the meditator. It can be as important a form of self-care as making sure we eat well, get enough sleep, and keep our body healthy. At the same time daily meditation may prepare us to care for others in calmer, wiser and more compassionate ways.

At other times it is appropriate to care for others; their needs may be greater than our own. On a particular day, we may have to skip our meditation session to tend to someone who needs our time or attention. One task of mindfulness practice, however, is to help us care for others without giving in to attitudes and reactions that undermine us, such as anxiety, stress, and over involvement. It is through careful attention that we learn how to benefit others without harming ourselves.

To understand Buddhist practice as a life of mutual benefit is to clearly place our practice within the context of our social life. Even if we spend long periods of time in mostly solitary practice, there is always a social dimension to our practice. We don't walk the path of liberation for ourselves only. Quite simply, by benefiting others we help ourselves, and by benefiting ourselves we serve and support others. We practice for the sake of all beings.

4

First Factor: Right View

People threatened by fear go to many refuges:
    To mountains, forests, parks, trees, and shrines.
None of these is a secure refuge; none is a supreme refuge.
    Not by going to such a refuge is one released
from all suffering.
But when someone, going for refuge to the Buddha, Dharma,
and Sangha
Sees, with right insight, the Four Noble Truths:
    Suffering,
    The arising of suffering,
    The overcoming of suffering,
    And the Eightfold Path leading to the ending of
    suffering,
Then this is the secure refuge; this is the supreme refuge.
By going to such a refuge one is released from all suffering.
         — *the Buddha (Dhammapada, v. 188-192)*

Behind almost everything we do, say, and think are views, some conscious and many not so conscious. Our views are the orientations, perspectives, and beliefs with which we understand our self and our world. They are the basis on which we choose how to live our lives. Often our core views are so embedded and habitual that they are not seen, and if they are known it is not as views but rather as the way things truly are.

Not all our views serve us. Many of the views, opinions,

beliefs, and stories we live by are the basis for our suffering. To counter this, the Eightfold Path begins with Right View. This is a perspective or frame of reference that provides a simple, straightforward understanding of how to bring suffering to an end. Part of the great value of Right View is the direct and pragmatic way it shows the path to inner freedom. It points us to our direct experience, which is an important alternative to basing our life on what we cannot know for ourselves.

Buddhism emphasizes two forms of Right View. One is the standpoint that what we do, say, and think doesn't exist in a vacuum. Rather these have physical and psychological consequences that are related to their ethical nature; if they are based on greed and hate, the consequences will be harmful. If they are based on generosity and kindness, the consequences will be beneficial. Whether or not this is borne out 100 percent of the time, I think it is certainly true that if we live by this view, we are more likely to think, speak, and act in ways that bring us and others greater well-being.

The second kind of Right View is the perspective of the Four Noble Truths. These are four useful perspectives for finding greater freedom and happiness. If we want to suffer less, it helps to notice when we are suffering (the First Noble Truth); it's all too easy to be distracted from suffering by other preoccupations. These distractions don't get rid of suffering, they just cover it over, like papering over cracks in a wall. It's also useful to discover the attachments that create the suffering (the Second Noble Truth) so we can begin to let go of them. The understanding that it is possible to let go of these attachments fully and thereby end suffering (the Third Noble Truth) gives direction and encouragement that we can do so. And finally, knowing a way to create the appropriate conditions for freeing ourselves from our clinging (the fourth Noble Truth) orients us to the practices that can help, namely the Eightfold Path.

Integral to the Four Noble Truths is the idea that if we want to become free of suffering, it is helpful to notice what causes our suffering. If we want to overcome suffering but don't know where to look for its cause, we might pursue beliefs, practices, and external remedies that have nothing to do with the problem. The Four Noble Truths direct us to find the cause within ourselves. While conventionally and sometimes appropriately we might say that someone or some event in the world caused our suffering, the Buddhist path to liberation begins when we start to take responsibility for what our inner, psychological contribution is to the suffering. In particular, the Four Noble

Truths point to the role of compulsive desires and cravings in giving birth to our inner suffering.

The Eightfold path begins with Right View because this is the view that puts us on the Buddha's path to liberation. If we want to find the path, Right View teaches us that it makes sense to take responsibility for our actions and that if we want to be free of suffering we can view our actions and experience through the perspective of the Four Noble Truths.

Right View also guides us and safeguards us in practicing the other seven factors of the Eightfold Path. It guides us by keeping the purpose of the Eightfold Path in mind, namely liberation from suffering. It safeguards us when it reveals any suffering and attachment that may come from the way we practice the other path factors. When we become aware of them we have the opportunity to let go of these attachments and find a more useful approach to practicing.

Using the Four Noble Truths as the view for understanding our life is a lot about practicing with ease. By ease, I mean a felt sense of well-being and inner freedom. The more at ease we become, the simpler it is to notice suffering, its cause, its cessation, and the path to its cessation. The more we use the Four Noble Truths to overcome attachments, the more we live at ease.

When people mature on the Buddhist path, the ease they experience becomes strong enough to naturally highlight the Four Noble Truths in their lives. An analogy is a white cloth—the cleaner the cloth becomes, the more obvious a new stain is. For this reason there is a long tradition of understanding the Buddhist phrase *cattāriariyasaccāni,* not as the "Four Noble Truths" but rather as the "Four Truths of the Noble Ones." The grammar of the phrase allows for both meanings. For those who use the truths as a wise view to live and practice, the four can be called the "Noble Truths"; for those who have experienced the peace of walking the path, they become a natural view to live by and so become the "Truths of the Noble Ones." Either way, practicing Right View leads to the most profound and meaningful peace.

REFLECTIONS AND PRACTICES FOR RIGHT VIEW

Week 1 – Inventory of Views

Spend a week noticing the primary views, orientations, or beliefs you live by. It could be useful to consider what, if any, deep, unnoticed views may underlie the more obvious ones. What role do views have in your life? What is your relationship to them? Which views do you have that are not beneficial for you? Which views are beneficial? What views do you most want to use to guide your life? Do you tend to operate on views you prefer not to base you life on? As you consider these questions it can be useful to write them down in a journal and then go back to re-read and re-consider what you wrote.

Behind many views is some desire that motivates you to have a view. You might reflect on what these desires are. Are the desires and wishes that motivate your views helpful or not?

Week 2 – Keeping Ease in View

For this exercise it may be useful to understand the difference between ease and relaxation. Relaxation has more to do with the lessening of tension and stress; it is felt in contrast to tension. Ease has more to do with an inner peace and harmony that exists without any reference to tension; it is felt more as something that exists in-and-of-itself. Relaxation is a relief, ease is a state of being.

This exercise asks you to notice the times you have some sense of ease. Notice the small moments of ease that appear briefly throughout your day, perhaps even during stressful occasions. If you know how to bring more ease into your life, during this week do so to whatever extent possible. What do you learn from this focus on ease? What does it highlight about your lack of ease?

Week 3 – Reflecting on Liberation

The Buddhist Right View is not a cosmic imperative to believe some truth. Rather it is a down-to-earth perspective that supports the goal of liberation from suffering, often called "awakening." What range of beliefs might you have about liberation or awakening? Which of these beliefs support practicing on the path to liberation? Which undermine the practice? How important is the possibility of reducing and ending suffering for you? Are you motivated by other goals that may interfere with focusing on the path to overcoming suffering? What ordinary or small experiences of liberation from suffering do you have in your daily life? What role can these have in supporting your practice? Please spend a week reflecting repeatedly on these questions. If possible, have a conversation with a friend about them.

Week 4 – Questions about Right View

Then during this week, formulate as many questions as you can about the Right View factor of the Eightfold Path. These can be questions about the traditional teachings and questions about yourself in relationship to Right View. After a week of daily reflection on questions, write down the three questions that are most compelling for you. Then share and discuss your questions with someone else.

5

Second Factor: Right Intention

"Intention, I tell you, is an action. Through intention one acts by way of body, speech, and mind."

—*The Buddha (Connected Discourses VI 63)*

The Buddha's approach to liberation can live within us when we understand the practices of the Eightfold Path. This path contains a remarkable set of straightforward practices that can free us from attachment and clinging and thus from suffering. As we saw in our discussion of Right View, it is the task of the first factor of the Eightfold Path to provide the perspective for finding the path by bringing our attention to suffering, its cause, and the possibility of ending it.

If we are interested in walking the Buddha's path to freedom, then Right View can show us whether our intentions are in accord with the purpose of this path. By applying the perspective of Right View to the intentions we live by we can determine if our intentions either cause suffering or contribute to its cessation. It is not possible to end suffering if our intentions cause suffering to others or ourselves.

Intentions are the primary or underlying motivations for what we think, say, or do. They are often more basic than what we want; they are the deeper purposes for why we want what we want. So, for example, we may want to go food shopping. The underlying intention might be to care for ourselves or our family, or the impetus to shop may be to distract ourselves from being lonely. Often, multiple intentions operate together. In shopping for groceries we might be motivated by wishes to eat healthily, to save money, to buy fair trade products, to impress friends coming to a dinner party, to be comforted, or to have pleasure. If we only think our intention is to shop, we may not consider these other purposes that inform why and how we shop.

Intentions are consequential. When we act on them, the consequences are found in their impact on the world. Whether we act on them or not, intentions also have an impact on our inner world of mind and heart. They contribute to our mood and to the quality of our mental life. Ongoing intentions create habits of mind that predispose us to continue to be motivated by these intentions. When intentions undermine our well being, they do so even more when they are habits. When intentions that support our happiness become second nature, we create the conditions for greater happiness.

In the Eightfold Path the Buddha singled out three

intentions or attitudes that cause suffering—and which take us away from the path. These are lust, ill will, and hostility (*kāma*, *vyāpāda*, and *himsa*). Lust—and this includes craving and addiction to sensual pleasures of any kind—reinforces attachment and keeps the mind agitated. Similarly, anyone who has experienced ill will and hostility knows these are troubled and painful states. By leading to more suffering, not less, lust, ill will, and hostility travel opposite the direction of the Eightfold Path.

In contrast, the second step on the Eightfold Path—Right Intention—involves cultivating intentions that do lead to less suffering. These are the positive opposites of lust, ill will, and hostility that can overcome these harmful motivations. The opposite of lust is described as renunciation or relinquishment (*nekkhama*). We can be inspired to practice wise renunciation when we consider its benefits: simplicity, ease, and non-harming. The opposites of ill will and hostility are non–ill will and non-hostility (*avyāpāda* and *ahimsa*). In the ancient language of the Buddha the negative prefix implies their positive opposites. Non–ill will means goodwill, and non-hostility means compassion.

In order to cultivate renunciation, goodwill, and compassion we begin by having the intention to do so. When it isn't easy to have good intentions, it's helpful and meaningful to wish that we could. Then we can at least practice restraint and not act on our harmful intentions.

If our intentions or thoughts involve lust, ill will, or hostility, then it is useful to find a way to disengage from them. Becoming aware of how painful these states are can help overcome the mind's obsession with them. If we recognize the value of the opposite of these intentions—renunciation, goodwill, and compassion—then it will be easier to adjust our orientation and think in terms of the positive intentions, even when we don't feel like it.

Here is an example of how this might work. When we are caught up in red-hot anger or frustration it is easy to have our attention preoccupied with what has triggered the anger. If we are overly preoccupied with the object of our anger, we may not be aware of what it feels like subjectively to be angry. But by becoming mindful of the subjective feeling of discomfort we can realize that it is not worthwhile to keep feeling this way. This helps us to lessen our interest in being preoccupied—after all, being preoccupied is not inherent in a difficult situation, it is part of our reaction to it. As preoccupation lessens we can reflect on useful ways to relate to the situation or the persons we are angry with. If we consider Right Intention we reflect on how goodwill or kindness might be useful. Practicing

Right Intention would mean finding ways to express this goodwill.

Reflecting on the three right intentions is not meant to pretend or to cover over what we really feel. Once we have become aware of how we feel then part of a realistic assessment of a situation includes considering the role that our intentions might have in that situation. In what way could the three right intentions be useful? Which one is most helpful? Through such consideration it becomes more likely that we will want to act on right intentions.

The intentions we live by have major consequences in shaping our lives, character, and psychological well-being. It is therefore invaluable to reflect deeply about what intentions are most important to us. These can be the compass directions that guide our lives. Even when it is a challenge to follow the compass, the wish to do so puts us on the path of liberation.

And what about those times we can't change our intentions for the better? In those cases it's useful to first bring a heightened awareness to these intentions. It is also helpful to be mindful of the relationships and reactivity we have to our unskillful intentions. Practicing non-judgmental mindfulness can reduce the suffering that comes from how we relate to these unskillful intentions straightforwardly without being reactive and adding to them. In applying Right Intentions to our unwise and unskillful intentions, we can arouse a degree of compassion for ourselves. We can also try to pause long enough to reflect on which intentions we do want to act on. Even if we have a strong desire to do something unskillful, we might be able to at least not act on the desire, we can act on something more skillful.

As was stated earlier, we don't just walk the Eightfold Path for ourselves. Sometimes people assume that in bringing attention to our suffering, the Eightfold Path leads only to self-concern. But the renunciation, goodwill, and compassion of Right Intention usually establish the path of practice within the context of our interpersonal relationships. A concern for the welfare of others is integral to walking the Eightfold Path. While it is the practice of Right Intention that fosters positive intentions toward others, the next three steps on the Eightfold Path—Right Speech, Right Action, and Right Livelihood—are about putting these intentions into action.

REFLECTIONS AND PRACTICES: RIGHT INTENTION

Week 1 – Lust and Renunciation

For this week give yourself time to notice and reflect on the role of lust in your life. For this purpose consider lust as any strong desire or compulsion for sensual pleasure of any kind. How much time do you spend thinking about and wanting sensual pleasure? What forms of sensual pleasure are you most motivated by? How do your desires for sensual pleasure affect you? How much time and money do you spend pursuing comfort, pleasure, or sensual gratification? How does your pursuit of sensual pleasure affect others?

Spend an equal amount of time considering what benefits might be available to you if you let go of attachments you may have to any sensual pleasure. What helpful intentions might you want to use to replace intentions connected to sensual pleasure? When you do pursue sensual pleasures, what other helpful intentions can guide this pursuit? In what ways can peace and simplicity help you understand the benefits of renunciation?

Week 2 – Ill Will and Goodwill

For this week notice and reflect on the role of ill will and aversion in your life. How frequently are you aversive, condemning, hateful, or indignant? In what conditions are you more likely to be aversive? How do aversion and ill will affect your body? How do they affect your mind and inner life? And how do they influence your behavior?

Also reflect on your relationship to goodwill, kindness, and loving-kindness. How often do you have goodwill for others? Are you interested in or motivated to have more goodwill? For this week spend time actively intending goodwill to others. This could be privately thinking thoughts of well-wishing to strangers you meet, e.g. store clerks, people in line with you, or the person standing in a line in front of you. It could be done by reflecting on how you might bring more friendliness to friends or relatives you will be spending time with. As you practice such good-will, how does this affect you?

Week 3 – Hostility and Compassion

For this week give yourself time to reflect on the ways hostility appears in your life. It may be useful to consider expressions of anger and irritation toward others or your-self as forms of hostility. Do your actions and words cause harm, even in minor ways? How are you harmed, perhaps mentally, when you express hostility? As you consider the effects of your hostility, how are you affected by this reflection?

Also reflect on your relationship to compassion. What role has compassion had in your life, both the receiving of it and having it for others? During this week, look for opportunities to experience compassion. Spend time staying with any compassion you might be feeling. How does it feel to be compassionate? How might it benefit you if you cultivated more compassion? How can you have more self-compassion?

During this week look for opportunities to act compassionately. Notice how acting with compassion affects you. In what ways can you act compassionately so that you feel more peaceful, more at ease, and perhaps less self-centered? How can compassion serve as a support to your inner freedom?

Week 4 – Loving-kindness Practice

During this week practice a period of loving-kindness meditation every day. If you are not familiar with this practice, instruction can be found in chapter 22 of my book, *The Issue at Hand*. In addition, as you go about your day, periodically send loving-kindness toward people you encounter. Consider ways you might like to act in kind ways; then try to do so.

6

Third Factor: Right Speech

A statement endowed with five factors is

> *well-spoken, not ill-spoken, blameless and not faulted by wise people.*

Which five?

> *It is spoken at the right time. It is spoken in truth. It is spoken politely. It is spoken beneficially. It is spoken with a mind of good-will.*

—*The Buddha (Anguttara Nikaya V.198)*

Right Intention, the second factor of the Eightfold Path, sets the stage for the next three factors, Right Speech, Right Action, and Right Livelihood. Grouped together as practices of virtue, these three factors are concerned with how the intentions of wise renunciation, goodwill, and compassion are expressed in our daily lives. These virtue factors also lay the foundation for the last three practices of the path—Right Effort, Right Mindfulness, and Right Concentration.

In starting with Right Speech, the three virtue practices begin with the activity through which we interact most with others and with which we most frequently impact others directly. What we say and how we say it also have a direct link to our own cultivation of the path of liberation. When we mindlessly speak or remain silent we lose an opportunity to include our speech as part of the Eightfold Path.

Right Speech is described as both speaking what is skillful and abstaining from speech that is unskillful. Lying, slandering, and engaging in harsh or pointless speech are defined as unskillful. Words that are honest, timely, useful, friendly, and create social harmony are considered wise and skillful.

Practicing Right Speech requires a dedication to mindfulness, especially to being aware of the impulse to speak before we actually speak. One approach for doing this is to develop the custom of pausing before speaking, perhaps a pause short enough to go unnoticed by others. This pause may give us the time to realize what we are intending to say. Knowing this may be enough for us to refrain from saying something we would later regret.

When we are uncertain what is skillful to say, it can be useful to consider the Buddha's guidelines for speech:

To speak at the appropriate time,

To speak honestly,

To speak politely,

To speak what is beneficial,

To speak with good will.

It is best to avoid speaking at a time when what we say can't be understood or when it is not useful for the person we are speaking to. Even if something is true and important, it is best to wait for the appropriate situation to say it.

Dishonesty takes us in the opposite direction from a path to liberation. Because the goal is to become truthful and authentic in all we do, dishonesty blocks the path to the goal. Honesty, in contrast, is mindfulness out loud. When combined with the other five guidelines, honesty creates trust and ease in everyone.

Politeness is respectful speech that expresses respect for others. Instead of demeaning or belittling others, polite speech enhances the dignity of both the person spoken to and the speaker.

Speaking only what is beneficial saves a lot of time and effort. Not only does it free us from having to say things that have no value or useful purpose, it also frees us from having to make amends for speech that is not beneficial, that brings pain.

Speaking with goodwill means to speak in ways that are kind and concerned with the welfare of others. Without goodwill, the heart will remain closed or numb. With goodwill, our speech supports the continuing opening of our hearts.

What we say has a powerful relationship to how we feel. The uncomfortable inner states that give rise to unskillful speech are strengthened by unskillful speech. One reason to avoid such speech is to avoid the agitation that comes with regret. Conversely, a reason to engage in skillful speech is to create conditions for happiness and peace. The inner well-being that supports skillful speech is strengthened by skillful speech.

When it is difficult to speak skillfully it may be possible to at least restrain ourselves from saying things that will cause harm. Avoiding unhelpful speech prevents a great amount of social discord and injury. At times, one of the most powerful, challenging, and wise practices we can do is to simply hold our tongue.

Abstaining from unskillful speech is not an end in itself, however. If we want to cultivate the freedom of the Eightfold Path it can be useful to investigate the inner conditions that motivate such speech. What does it teach us about ourselves? Are we overly stressed? Are we being unduly influenced by desire, aversion, or fear? What are we trying to accomplish through such speech? If we could settle deeply into our hearts, what would we say?

And even if we succumb to our unskillful impulses and engage in unwise speech, we can still gain valuable insight into ourselves. Considering whether or not our speech expresses goodwill, friendliness, or compassion can be the beginning of practicing Right Speech. If we find that our speech doesn't have these qualities, then we have a golden opportunity to find out why. What does such speech show us about ourselves? If we truly care about ourselves, then reflecting on these questions can inspire us to find alternate ways of speaking. Rather than being discouraging or providing occasions to beat ourselves up, such self-knowledge can fuel our practice.

These kinds of reflections are useful so that we don't practice Right Speech simply as a set of rules, but as a way to support our practice on the path. These investigations help us get in touch with our inner life and the inner wellsprings of wisdom and caring from which we can better consider what to say. It is good to remember that our speech arises out of the ecology of our inner life. If the inner life is well cared for it is much easier to speak wisely. By practicing Right Speech we are not only cultivating the Eightfold Path, but we are also taking care of both others and ourselves. Right Speech benefits the world and strengthens our path of liberation.

Reflections and Practices: Right Speech

Week 1 – The Experience of Speaking

One of the most challenging but also rewarding areas of mindfulness practice is mindful speech. If we tune in to ourselves, we can experience the relationship speaking has to our bodies, our emotional lives, our beliefs and ideas, our preferences, and the ways our life experiences have conditioned us. Please spend a week being mindful of these areas when you speak. It might be helpful to keep a journal recording what you notice. You might find the following sequence helpful:

Day one: Focus on noticing what is happening in your body as you speak.

Day two: Focus on how you feel emotionally when you speak.

Day three: Focus on noticing what motivates you to speak. Why do you say what you do?

Day four: Be mindful of what you are paying attention to when you speak. Are you focused on your words? Do you pay attention to the people you're talking to? How aware of your body are you as you speak?

Day five: Keep your attention anchored in your body as you speak. Notice how this affects what you say.

Day six and seven: Repeat some of the practices from the first five days.

Week 2 – Honesty

This week's exploration of truthful speech has two parts, listening well and speaking honestly.

Spend the first few days of this week devoted to listening to others more carefully than you usually do. How does this affect what you say? As you listen, notice what inner dialogue you might have. Are you rehearsing what you will say? Are you commenting on what you are hearing? Do you get easily distracted by unrelated thoughts?

Spend the rest of the week noticing what it's like to be honest and what it's like when you are anything less than honest. Perhaps in most conversations this is not a particularly important issue because honesty is easy. However, what does it feel like when honesty is not so easy? Or when the honesty is an important part of the communication? What does it feel like when you are avoiding honest communication? What motivates this avoidance? If you find yourself saying something that is not truthful, spend some time investigating why and how you did this.

Find a person you can talk to about the role of honesty in conversation. You might ask them what they have learned in their life about speaking truthfully.

Week 3 – Social Harmony and Speech

When the Buddha advised us to avoid slanderous speech, he also encouraged us to speak so we can unite those who are divided and encourage those who are united. During this week, give special attention to saying things that create social harmony and concord. Avoid speaking badly about anyone. Instead look for natural and appropriate opportunities to speak well about others, including the people you are with. Notice how you are affected by speaking in such ways.

Week 4 – Motivations to Speak

During this week notice why you say what you say. What motivations are behind what you do and don't say? Notice the strength of your impulses to speak. What affects the strength of this impulse? When you are mindful of your motivation and impulses to speak, how does this affect what you say?

When you know you will be speakng to someone, prepare yourself by reflecting on what intentions you might want for the conversation. How does a conversation unfold if you have reflected and set an intention beforehand?

During some of your conversations this week practice "pausing and relaxing" before you speak. Don't rush in to contribute to a conversation. Take a moment to pause and relax before you speak. Notice how this affects what you say and how you say it.

Choose some conversations during this week in which you can emphasize saying things that are pleasing, heartwarming, and meaningful for the people you are speaking with. Notice how this affects you.

7

Fourth Factor: Right Action

*"There are these five gifts, great gifts, primal, of long stand-
ing, traditional, ancient. What five? Abstaining from harming life, from taking what is not given, from sexual misconduct, from false speech, from liquor, wine, and intoxicants
that are the basis for heedlessness.*

—*The Buddha (Anguttara Nikaya 8:38)*

The intention to avoid causing harm lies at the heart of
the entire Eightfold Path. In fact, without it there is no
Eightfold Path. The practice of avoiding harm through
our physical actions is the fourth path factor, Right
Action. This factor is most commonly defined as not
engaging in specific activities. The tasks of Right Action
are to avoid three specific things:

- killing any sentient being
- taking anything belonging to others that is not
  freely given
- engaging in sexual misconduct

Practicing these three restraints can be inspiring when
we consider the safety and peace they create both for others and for ourselves. In a world where too many people
are in danger of physical harm, practicing right action supports peace.

The dedication to not killing can be interpreted more

broadly so it precludes causing any physical harm to others. This may well have been the Buddha's original intent because the word translated as killing, *patipata*, also means to attack and to injure. The avoidance of killing and injuring pertains to all conscious, breathing beings, not only other humans. It includes insects, pests, and the slaughter of animals for food. While the Buddha did not prescribe vegetarianism, he forbade his monastic disciples from eating meat if the animal was killed specifically in order to feed them.

Avoiding taking what is not given is a higher standard than simply not stealing. It means we don't take, borrow, or use anything belonging to others unless it has been specifically offered to us. It also implies that we do not withhold items in our possession that rightfully belong to others. It includes cheating on one's taxes or using more natural resources like water, electricity, etc., than might reasonably be considered "given freely."

To refrain from sexual misconduct is to avoid any sexual activity with others that might cause harm. It means taking great care not to hurt our sexual partners. It also means respecting and upholding all relationship commitments that have been made, including those made by others.

When we avoid injuring others we also avoid injuring

ourselves. When we practice Right Action, for example, we're less likely to have a painful conscience. In addition, the less harm we cause, the less likely it is that others will be angry with us or wish to retaliate with hurtful behaviors towards us. Right Action also prevents us from acting on our impulses of greed, hate, or delusion. This, in turn, protects us from experiencing the negative consequences that come from acting on these underlying motivations.

Living without intentionally harming any living being is also a source of happiness called the "bliss of blamelessness." This is an ease in the mind from being free of any reason to be reproached, either by oneself or by others. The absence of remorse, fear, and criticism is something to appreciate. It is a joy that can grow from reflection on a mind that has a clear conscience. A mind with a clear conscience is conducive for meditation practice.

Hate is a common motivation for wanting to injure or kill; greed is often behind stealing; sexual misconduct can have a variety of motivations. In addition killing, stealing and sexual misconduct all contain a degree of delusion, in particular the delusion of not recognizing the harmful consequences that can ensue. Greed, hate, and delusion may all be entangled with fear—and they arise sometimes as responses to fear. Right Action is a way to help us limit the impact of these painful motivations.

Because it can be easier to control our actions than to control our mind, the three abstinences of Right Action can be an effective way of preventing greed, hate, and delusion from controlling us. When any of these three are strong, not acting on them may require marshaling a matching degree of restraint. But it is worth it. Restraint as a form of Right Action keeps these impulses in check in such a way that mindfulness can then help us understand, resolve, and dissolve them from the inside without harming others or causing further harm to ourselves.

In addition to these practices of restraint, Right Action also includes acting on the opposite motivations. Instead of greed, we can tap into our capacity for generosity; instead of hate, we might cultivate love and respect for others; instead of delusion, we might take time to pay more careful attention to the people and beings we encounter.

We can be prompted to cultivate positive motivations when we encounter greed, hate, and delusion in ourselves. If we feel an urge to injure others we can instead consider the situation through the perspective of compassion. The impulse to take what is not given might instead prompt an exploration of contentment. Any time there is a desire for

a sexual relationship is probably a good time to ask if compassion and respect are adequately present; this is even
more important when we are motivated to engage in sexual misconduct.

Some people prefer to emphasize the positive sides of
Right Action—what they can do rather than what they
should avoid—because they don't feel inspired by the
avoidance of killing, stealing, and sexual misconduct.
Sometimes people can feel burdened by the seemingly
restrictive nature of these teachings. Even so, one advantage of the negative formulation of these practices is that it
is often easier to determine which behaviors constitute
non-injuring, non-killing, non-stealing, or sexual misconduct than it is to decide how to be compassionate, gener-
ous, and respectful.

Ideally the negative and positive sides of Right Action
work together. When we restrain harmful actions, we have
the opportunity to consider and cultivate behaviors that
promote well-being for ourselves and others. For example,
practicing non-killing may help us cultivate a greater
appreciation for life; practicing non-stealing may help us
cultivate respect for others, and practicing good sexual
conduct may help us cultivate trustworthiness.

In addition, it is important to appreciate the tremendous value of looking deeply into the motivations and feelings behind our actions. For practitioners on the Eightfold Path, Right Action provides an opportunity to bring greater mindfulness to the underlying causes of unskillful behavior. In this way, Right Action works together with the first two factors of the path, Right View and Right Intention. Plus, it can be inspiring to know that practicing the Eightfold Path is a way to release ourselves from these underlying painful and potentially destructive roots of greed, hate, and delusion.

REFLECTIONS AND PRACTICES: RIGHT ACTION

Week 1 – Intentions for Action

While you may rarely, if ever, act on intentions to cause harm, do you have thoughts, wishes, or impulses toward others that would cause harm if acted upon? Do you have impulses for revenge, retribution, or animosity toward others? Do you ever have thoughts or fantasies about taking things not given or taking more than is offered? Do you scheme about how you can get something before someone else gets it? Do you take advantage of people's time and goodwill? Do you have thoughts, fantasies, or desires for sexual relations with inappropriate people?

During this week be attentive to these kinds of intentions and thoughts. How often do you have them? In what circumstances are you most likely to have them? What attitudes do you have toward these intentions? Is there an underlying motivation, need, or personal situation that is fuel for these intentions?

During this week, also spend some time putting yourself in other people's shoes; imagine yourself in their situation. How might this shift the intentions you have toward others?

Week 2 – Not Killing or Harming

Do you have exceptions to the precept of not killing? Do you have justifications or rationales for when it is okay to kill people, animals, or pests? What are these justifications? In what situations are you committed to not killing or not injuring other people or nonhuman beings? What motivates this commitment?

How does it benefit you and your Buddhist or mindfulness practice to be committed to not killing? Are there ways you can expand on this commitment?

For the Buddha, having compassion for all beings is the alternative to killing or harming. During this week, find ways to increase the compassion you feel toward others. You might read my article "Cultivating Compassion," which can be found on the Articles page of IMC's website (insightmeditationcenter.org).

Week 3 – Not Taking What Is Not Given

Are there things you take that are not given? Do you help yourself to things and/or free time at work that have not been offered? Are there situations in your life where you exert inappropriate authority over others, coerce people to do things they don't want, or take more of their time than they have offered? Are there any, even subtle, areas where you are liable to take what has not been given?

Spend some time reflecting on all of these questions. What motivates them? What beliefs support them? How often do you engage in these behaviors because you're feeling lazy or unwilling to spend the time to do the right thing?

How does not taking what is not given apply to your use of natural resources? Are such natural resources you use like water, energy of various sources, or the source materials for the goods you use "freely given?" Are they freely given in unlimited supply? Do you believe these are given because we can buy them?

Spend two days this week reflecting on the precept of not taking what is not given. Then spend two more days practicing not taking what is not given as thoroughly as you possibly can. You might go as far as some Buddhist monastics do who will not pick up a book on someone's coffee table unless there is a clear invitation to do so. Don't force yourself forward in traffic. If you need something and it is not offered, ask for it or examine whether you really need it.

For the next two days, focus on practicing generosity. Look for opportunities to give things, time, compliments, the benefit of the doubt, and other acts of kindness. At the end of the week review and compare the practice of abstaining from taking what is not given with the practice of generosity. How were the challenges and benefits similar or different?

Week 4 – Not Engaging in Sexual Misconduct

One way or another sexual desire and expression are part of everyone's life, at the very least in contending with social expectations around sexuality. It is well worth reflecting deeply about our own relationship to our sexuality. The questions that follow are meant for your own private reflections:

What role and influence does sexual desire have in your life? Is the influence beneficial for you? In the context of Right Action, are you comfortable with your sexuality? If not, what would it take to become comfortable with it? What is your understanding of sexual misconduct? Are there forms of thinking, fantasizing, and solitary activities that you engage in that involve sexual misconduct? If you are involved with any of these, what might be satisfying and realistic ways of substituting appropriate sexual conduct for them?

During this week, spend some time bringing a heightened sense of respect to the person or people you have sexual feelings or thoughts about. Devote time, perhaps two sessions of meditation, to practicing loving-kindness toward them. What effect does this respect and loving-kindness have on your sexual desires and thoughts?

8

Fifth Factor: Right Livelihood

And what is right livelihood? This is when a disciple of the noble ones, having abandoned dishonest livelihood, keeps his life going with right livelihood: This is called right livelihood.

—the Buddha *(Connected Discourses 45.8)*

In moving along the Eightfold Path from Right Action to Right Livelihood, we switch from a focus on our particular actions to focusing on the general ways in which we live our lives. In general, the things we do repeatedly have much greater consequences than the things we do only once or a few times. The effects may ripple further out into our society and deeper into our hearts.

Right Livelihood is the most common English translation of the Buddhist expression *sammā-ājīva*. However, because *ājīva* means the way one lives, it encompasses more than one's job or occupation. It includes such lifestyle choices as what we buy, consume, use for housing, and rely on for financial support. It also includes how we parent, care for our family, or live in retirement. When walking the Eightfold Path the question regarding Right Livelihood is whether or not the way we live moves us toward more compassion, peace, and freedom. Is it nourishing? Does it support the development of ease and insight? Does it help us become a better, happier person? Does it help others?

Behind these questions is the fundamental question that guides us along each step of the Eightfold Path: Is what we are doing causing harm to others or suffering for ourselves? When this is applied to Right Livelihood, we ask whether the way we live and the way we support ourselves cause harm or suffering. If the answer is yes, then we remind ourselves that this is at cross-purposes with a path meant to end suffering and harm.

When considering whether our way of life negatively impacts others, we can take into account how we contribute to the aggregate effect of many other people doing the same activity. If we were the only person driving a car on the roads, for example, the exhaust we produce would have little or no effect on the health of others. But when we are one of the five million drivers in the San Francisco Bay Area we are contributing to the smog-related health problems both in the Bay Area, and in the central valley where the smog often drifts. Similarly, when millions of people install additional electrical equipment to their homes or carelessly discard their old computers and cell phones, the aggregate effect has repercussions far beyond what we can see in our immediate, individual lives. An action that might not be very harmful if only one person does it can become detrimental when many people do it.

Such considerations aren't meant to evoke anxiety and guilt. Rather they are meant to motivate us to find a way to live that increases our ease and peace and benefits our community. Right Livelihood is a practice that cultivates greater awareness and responsibility for the world while being less weighed down by remorse, concern that we are causing too much unintended harm, or sense of ethical unease.

For many people the most significant aspect of Right Livelihood is the work they do. Many people spend more time working than any other activity except perhaps sleeping. Work and other occupations such as parenting are often the vehicle through which people have their biggest impact on others. When considering whether our work constitutes Right Livelihood, we can ask whether it harms other people or ourselves. If our work or the way in which we do our work clearly has a negative impact, then we are not walking the Eightfold Path with our livelihood.

Considering our work through the lens of Right Livelihood can be a meaningful contemplation on what is most important to us. What are the purposes for which we work? What values do we express in our work? What consequences does our work have on the quality of our inner life? What consequences does it have on the world? If we are on the path of liberation, does our work and the way we go about it further us on this path?

Because joy, ease, and peace are important parts of the Buddhist path, the question of Right Livelihood includes considering whether we enjoy our work. Is the way we live our life satisfying and meaningful? If it isn't, what can we change to have greater joy, satisfaction, and meaning?

Many things help make our livelihood a source of enjoyment and satisfaction. Being honest and ethical in work is foundational. There can be no ease if one does not have a clean conscience. Doing work that benefits others is helpful, and so is sharing the fruits of our work with others. Living a balanced life and avoiding overworking supports ease and calm. Not being in debt is also important for ease of mind.

How we work also has a big effect. Being mindful, engaged, and focused in our work is more satisfying than being distracted and uninspired. This is also true when we enjoy the work for its own sake rather than for the income it will bring. Working with attitudes of generosity and kindness can create a more supportive work environment.

If we are trying to live by the Eightfold Path, the practice of Right Livelihood is dedicated to living and working in a way that supports the path. This is accomplished by practicing the first four factors of the Path in our working life. In particular this means to practice goodwill, compassion, Right Speech, and ethical behavior while we work. It also can include working in ways that support the last three practices of the Eightfold Path, Right Effort, Right Mindfulness, and Right Concentration.

When we practice the Eightfold Path at work, our tasks can become energizing, calming, and easeful. This in turn makes it much easier for us when we sit down to meditate. Meditation becomes less about de-stressing and relaxing and more about developing mindfulness and concentration. The result is a greater capacity to further fulfill the Eightfold Path at work.

Reflections and Practices: Right Livelihood

Week 1 – What We Produce

The primary activities we engage in to sustain our life are what constitute livelihood. These can be grouped into two categories: what we produce and what we consume. Production refers to what we create or engage in that provides us with the financial and material support for our life. Consumption pertains to what we buy and use in order to sustain our life and our lifestyle.

This week give special attention to what you produce. What work or activities do you engage in that provide you with financial and material support? If you are employed, what do you produce? If you are a homemaker, what are you making? If you are retired with investments, in what have you invested? If you are a student, are your studies directed toward being able to do something that will provide you with a livelihood? Do you believe this livelihood goal is Right Livelihood?

What is your relationship to what you produce? What attitudes do you have toward your work? Does it inspire you? If so, how? Is it meaningful? If so, how? Does it help you become a better person? Does it benefit others? Can you think of ways you benefit yourself and others through your work that you might be overlooking? What values do you express through the work you do? What values do you wish you better expressed at work?

Spend this week reviewing and reflecting on these questions. Discuss them with friends. Write down some of your answers. Please do this repeatedly so that you might begin to discover new perspectives on these questions.

Week 2 – What We Consume

What do you consume, use, buy, or spend your time doing in order to both meet your basic needs and sustain your lifestyle? What motivates the choices you make about what you consume? How are you affected by what you consume? What values are you expressing by these choices? What values do you wish were more a part of these choices? Does what you consume make you a better person? Does it benefit others in any direct or indirect way? Please spend the week delving as deeply as you can into these questions.

Wee 3 – Work and the Eightfold Path

For four days this week, consider how you can practice each of the first four factors of the Eightfold Path (Right View, Right Intention, Right Speech, and Right Action) in your livelihood, whether it is at a job, homemaking, studying, or in retirement. You might reread the chapters on these factors while considering how the teachings relate to your work life. Be sure to have a dialogue with someone about the relationship you see between work and each of these factors, so you might carry your reflections further than if you explored them on your own.

Week 4 – Consumption and the Eightfold Path

For four days this week, consider how you can practice each of the first four factors of the Eightfold Path in relation to what you consume, use, buy, or how you spend your time. For Right View, consider what happens when you look at your consumption through the lens of the Four Noble Truths. For Right Intention, explore how you might benefit from greater compassion, goodwill, and renunciation in your non-work related activities. For Right Speech, think about how you can do these activities with kinder and more honest speech. Are your patterns of consumption aligned with Right Action? Again, please find someone to discuss these reflections with.

9

Sixth Factor: Right Effort

It is for you to make strong effort
The Buddhas only tell you how.

(Dhammapada v. 276)

Right Effort, Right Mindfulness, and Right Concentration are the factors of the path that address our inner activities, what we do with our minds and hearts. This focus is distinct from the emphasis on verbal and physical activities in the three preceding factors: Right Speech, Right Action, and Right Livelihood. Attention to and care with our outward actions prepare us to do the same for our inner, mental actions. As with other factors on the path, what guides this care is the intention to avoid causing harm and to engage in what is beneficial for ourselves and others.

The Buddhist tradition often refers to activities that cause harm as unskillful and those that are beneficial as skillful. The use of these terms highlights the idea that we can choose to think, speak and act in ways that are beneficial. Using the words skillful and unskillful avoids the moralistic judgments that good and bad often imply, and the absoluteness of right and wrong. Skillfulness suggests "helpfulness"; things that are unskillful are simply not helpful. When one is walking the Eightfold Path, skillful activities are those that help us move closer to peace and freedom. Those that are unskillful take us in the other direction, toward suffering and servitude.

Distinguishing mental actions that are skillful from those that are not is at the heart of Right Effort. Here mental actions refer to the thoughts, impulses, feelings, and states that arise and persist, depending on our intentions and reactions. Only by recognizing whether or not these are helpful and beneficial can we usefully choose which thoughts, impulses, feelings, or states to cultivate and which ones not to, and where we want to put our efforts. In practicing Right Effort we exercise these choices to support the path of liberation.

Right Effort involves four different ways we can apply ourselves. When it comes to our inner thoughts, feelings, and states, we can (1) prevent, (2) abandon, (3) arouse, or (4) maintain these inner experiences. Far from being uniquely Buddhist practices, these four are common throughout human life. For example, when we avoid stress by giving ourselves ample time to get to an appointment, we are preventing; when we consciously relax our impatience while waiting for a red light to turn green, we are abandoning; when we cultivate appreciation of another person, we are arousing; and when we stay calm in difficult circumstances we are maintaining.

In the practice of Right Effort we utilize these four efforts to safeguard and develop the quality of our mind and heart. The quality of our inner life is our most important asset, and it deserves our utmost care. When we see clearly that unskillful mental states decrease the quality of our inner life, it is natural to want to either prevent these states from occurring or, if they are already there, to find a way to abandon them. And when we understand that there are things we can do to increase the quality of our inner life, it's healthy and makes sense to do so. In this way the quality of our inner life can be improved.

Preventing, the first of the four Right Efforts, involves avoiding and restraining. Avoiding means not putting ourselves in situations where unskillful mind states are bound to be triggered. For example, if we have an addiction, it's best to stay clear of the people, places, and things that will tempt us to indulge. If we tend to become angry when we're around angry people, maybe it's best to avoid those people. This effort to avoid is built on the understanding that we are better off without unskillful mental states and behaviors.

Restraining is the practice of not giving in to unskillful

reactions and desires. It requires first recognizing impulses and thoughts of greed, ill-will, and delusion when they arise, and then holding them in check so we neither act on them nor feed them with more mental involvement.

When unskillful states of mind are present in us, Right Effort involves abandoning them. At times, this can be done through a simple act of stopping or letting go of the unhelpful mental activity we're engaged in. We see what our mind is doing—judging another person, for example, or criticizing ourselves—and we decide to stop it. Other times, we can achieve this by first acquiring a good understanding of the mental state we want to overcome. Sometimes, insight into the conditions that give rise to the unskillful states can show us the underlying attachments to let go of.

The third Right Effort is arousing skillful mental states, thoughts, and intentions. These mental states are not only helpful on the path of liberation, they are also satisfying in themselves. Particularly useful are the seven factors of awakening: mindfulness, investigation, energy, joy, tranquility, concentration, and equanimity. Also helpful are loving-kindness, compassion, and appreciative joy. Some of these states arise as a consequence of meditation practice and some can be purposefully cultivated with other activities.

Once skillful states have arisen, the job of the fourth Right Effort is maintaining them. This includes recognizing and appreciating skillful states when they are present as well as applying the first Right Effort of preventing unskillful states from arising. Continuing the actions and practices that give rise to skillful states is also a way to maintain them.

In practicing these four Right Efforts, care should be taken to not avoid difficult feelings, thoughts, and mind states that would be better to focus on with mindful and compassionate attention. Sometimes the inner difficulties we are having can represent something that needs to be seen clearly or that is working itself out inside us. In such circumstances arousing good states of mind can inhibit or delay something that needs to be resolved.

Practicing with Right Effort can also include giving attention to the way in which we make effort. The kind of effort required varies depending on the circumstances— sometimes heroic effort is appropriate, and other times what's needed is an extremely light touch. It can happen that the purpose of our efforts is beneficial but the way we exert ourselves to attain this goal is not. For example, we can be too aggressive or too hesitant, too self-aggrandizing or too self-deprecating in the way we apply ourselves.

Our effort in Buddhist practice can be delightful when it is free of greed, aversion, and fear. At times effort can feel almost effortless and satisfying for its own sake. Certainly it can be inspiring to know our efforts are dedicated to walking the Eightfold Path, to bringing greater peace and freedom into this world.

REFLECTIONS AND PRACTICES: RIGHT EFFORT

Week 1 – The Effort of Preventing

This week, reflect on the states of mind, trains of thought, desires, and intentions you commonly experience that you would be better off without. Under what circumstances are these most likely to occur? What do you need to avoid in order to lessen the likelihood of these occurring? In what appropriate ways can you avoid the circumstances that tend to bring them up?

Choose to avoid one thing this week that you know is a catalyst for the arising of unskillful states in you. Notice the benefits and costs of practicing avoidance. What do you learn about yourself through doing this practice?

In addition, twice during the week spend a two-hour period of time practicing "safeguarding yourself at the sense doors." This is the practice of staying attentive enough to the stimulus you receive that you can avoid reacting negatively. When you perceive a sight, sound, smell, taste, or touch that could trigger an unskillful mental state, recognize clearly what you are perceiving while also watching yourself. In this way, you can avoid getting involved with unskillful reactions to what you are experiencing through your sense doors. This practice is most satisfying when it safeguards a state of mind that is peaceful, loving, or otherwise beneficial.

Week 2 – The Effort of Overcoming

Consider the following questions this week: When you are experiencing an unskillful mental state, what are your preferred ways of overcoming it, of causing it to go away? Are your methods healthy or unhealthy? Do your strategies come from wisdom or from aversion? How does your wisdom cast light on the practice of overcoming or abandoning unskillful states?

Notice when you are thinking unskillful thoughts—for instance, thoughts of resentment, ill-will, greed, covetousness, frightening imaginings about the future, or negative opinions about yourself or others. Once you notice them, practice letting these thoughts go. Apply skillful means to stop these trains of thinking. If you can't stop them, try to distract yourself from these concerns. When you are no longer having the unskillful thoughts notice how not having the thoughts feels different than having them. How does this affect your overall ability to think and evaluate wisely?

Week 3 – The Effort of Arousing

This week, make a list of three emotional states or attitudes that you think are worthwhile for you to cultivate.

What are the circumstances that tend to evoke these emotional states or attitudes in you? In what circumstances is it appropriate to intentionally arouse them? What wise ways do you know for arousing these states and attitudes? When is it beneficial to do this and when might it be counterproductive?

Choose one skillful state and spend an entire day cultivating it. This could be, for example, friendliness, joy, compassion, gratitude, generosity, calm, or equanimity. Plan ahead by picking a day when you know you'll have time to actively focus on this state. You might prepare by creating some reminders on Post-It notes to help you keep the quality in mind, and by selecting some short reflections or readings to look at throughout the day. At the end of the day, assess what you learned by regularly cultivating the state over the course of a day.

Week 4 – The Effort of Maintaining

What are some of the causes and conditions that lead you to lose touch with skillful mental states? For instance, if you're calm, how do you lose that calm? If you're happy, what causes it to fade? If you have goodwill for others, what undermines it? In contrast, what supports the continuation of these skillful states? What values, priorities, and intentions do you have that can support the continuation of skillful states? Which ones undermine them?

Choose a skillful state that you value and that you can easily evoke. This could be being relaxed before doing something that makes you anxious; it could be evoking curiosity to investigate something rather than prejudging it; or it could be bringing forth a basic friendliness when in a gathering of strangers. Establish the skillful state just before entering a situation in which you know it will be challenging to maintain the state. Experiment with making an effort to keep the state going throughout the situation. Afterwards, reflect on the effort you made. What can you learn about your effort? Was it wise? Were you able to find an appropriate way to maintain the skillful state? During this week, do this three times. Then, if you can, discuss your experiences with a friend.

10

Seventh Factor: Right Mindfulness

What is Right Mindfulness?

Here a practitioner abides focused on the body in itself, on feeling tones in themselves, on mental states in themselves, and on mental processes in themselves, ardent, clearly comprehending, and mindful, having put away greed and distress for the world.

—The Buddha (Middle Length Discourse 141.30)

When the steps of the Eightfold Path are practiced sequentially from Right View to Right Concentration, the journey of practice goes inward to the most intimate parts of our being. Right View and Right Intention provide the broad understanding for walking the path; Right Speech, Right Action, and Right Livelihood bring the practice home to our behavior in the world; Right Effort, Right Mindfulness, and Right Concentration take the practice into the heart, to our innermost capacity to experience peace and ease.

Right Mindfulness is more than simply being mindful. In the Buddha's ancient instructions, *sati*—the word often rendered into English as "mindfulness,"—refers to the presence of mind needed for a strong, balanced awareness. "Mindfulness practice" occurs when this presence of mind is combined with clear comprehension, ardency, and a willingness to put aside preoccupations with things of the world. And when this mindfulness practice is directed toward the four foundations of mindfulness it is known as Right Mindfulness.

Clear comprehension lies at the center of mindfulness practice. Whereas mindfulness allows us to be aware, clear comprehension understands whatever it is we're aware of. Because it's difficult to have clear understanding when we're in the grip of greed or distress, the instruction for mindfulness practice is to put these aside. When this is difficult to do, the practice requires us to at least let go of focusing on the thing we want or that distresses us. Instead, we begin tracking what is happening in our body, feeling tones, and mind in the face of our own greed or distress.

Practicing Right Mindfulness is a journey inward. Traditionally, Right Mindfulness involves attention to four progressively more refined and intimate areas of our lives. These four, usually called the "Four Foundations of Mindfulness" are:

- the body
- feeling tones
- mental states
- mental processes

The journey begins with establishing mindfulness of the body, including our breathing, physical activities, and physical sensations. After focusing on the body, we then establish mindfulness of the simple feeling tones of our direct, present-moment experiences.

The feeling tones are the most basic way we experience sensations as either pleasant, unpleasant, or neither pleasant nor unpleasant. As these tones come into focus it is possible to distinguish those that arise due to our contact with the outside world from those that, independent of the world, arise based on what is happening in our mind and heart. So, for example, sensations of sight, sound, smell, taste, and touch arise from contact with the sense world. Buddhism includes as part of this the inner experiences that only have a physical source.

Distinct from this are the sensations that do not arise from the stimulation of our five senses. These are sensations associated with mental states or moods. They are sensations that can occur independent of what is happening in our immediate environment. Meditation, for example, can produce pleasant sensations that have nothing to do with the sense world. In fact, it is possible to experience unpleasant physical sensations simultaneously with having the pleasure of meditative joy.

Being mindful of the distinction between experiences that arise from stimulation of our physical senses from those that arise from our mental states leads to a greater awareness of our mental states, which is the third foundation of mindfulness. Here, what is meant by a mental state is the overall mood or attitude of the mind. This refers to the overall emotional state of the mind as well as the way the mind can feel contracted or expansive, caught up or free.

With greater awareness of mental states, the journey of mindfulness leads to the fourth foundation of mindfulness. This is where we have a clear recognition of the mental processes operating in relation to our mental states.

This last foundation involves cultivating wisdom about what our minds do to cause suffering and what we can do to overcome this suffering. We learn to recognize the mental processes, such as the hindrances, that need to be let go of so we can realize a peaceful heart. It also includes recognizing and cultivating the seven mental process that support the mind to be expansive, tranquil, and liberated. These are mindfulness, investigation, energy, joy, tranquility, concentration, and equanimity. The last foundation also includes having a clear and "direct knowing" of the Four Noble Truths as insights that lead to liberation.

Reflections and Practices: Right Mindfulness

Week 1 – Mindfulness of the Body

What is your relationship to mindfulness of the body? Is it difficult for you to be aware of your body? How often do you practice mindfulness of your body? How is attention to your body beneficial? What are some of the lessons you learn through careful attention to your physical experience? In what areas of your life would it be useful for you to have more mindfulness of your body?

The traditional practice of mindfulness of the body begins by focusing on breathing and intentionally relaxing the body as you do so. Spend a period of time each day, outside of meditation, breathing mindfully and relaxing your body. Then engage in an ordinary daily activity while staying centered in awareness of your body, practicing mindfulness of your physical experience. What benefits come from doing this?

Week 2 – Mindfulness of Feeling Tones

Everything we experience falls into one of three "flavors." Something can be pleasant, unpleasant, or neither pleasant nor unpleasant. As you live your life, are you more affected by one of these three or do you tend to be influenced by all three equally? Which of the three has the most influence on your behavior? Which tends to agitate you the most? What are some of the beliefs you have about pleasure and pain? What wisdom do you have about relating to what is pleasant or unpleasant?

The traditional practice of mindfulness of feeling tones differentiates feelings that are "of the flesh" and those that are "not of the flesh." This may be understood as feelings that arise through our ordinary senses and those which occur independent of our senses and perceptions of the external world. Some people refer to the latter kind of feelings as "spiritual." Another way of thinking about this is that the second category refers to feelings associated with the quality of our inner life or inner emotional state.

During this week spend time nourishing your inner life. Rather than doing activities that bring you pleasure, do things that bring satisfaction, meaning, or happiness to your heart. As you do so, be mindful of any pleasure or pleasantness that arises in your heart or inner life.

Week 3 – Mindfulness of Mental States

Mental states are the general moods of our minds. When we repeatedly think or intend the same thing, it can condition the general disposition or quality of the mind. Sometimes this is obvious when we see people who are visibly displaying a mood. With mindfulness we can become skilled at recognizing the mental state of our own mind.

While changeable, mental states are not as fleeting as particular thoughts. Mental states tend to persist for a while. What are the three most common mental states you experience? What causes these states to arise? What causes them to persist? With causes them to pass away? What beliefs or stories do you tell yourself about your mental states? What influence do these mental states have on you and your behavior? What has been your experience of practicing mindfulness of your mental states?

A simple way of practicing mindfulness of mental states is to notice where your state of mind fits on a spectrum—from expanded, light, and open to contracted, heavy, and closed. As you go through the day take time to be clearly aware of where you are on this spectrum. Notice how and when you shift along this spectrum. Also take time to notice what your degree of expansiveness or contractedness feels like. What happens to you as you recognize and feel this aspect of your mental state?

Week 4 – Mindfulness of Mental Processes

Mindfulness of mental processes is a wisdom practice because it involves understanding the attitudes, beliefs, and mental behaviors that either bring inner freedom or lead us to be to become caught up in attachment. What are some of the reasons you get attached or obsessed? What are some of your attachments that you understand so well that letting go of them is relatively easy? What are some of the psychological benefits you have seen from letting go? What are some of your stronger attachments, the ones you can only let go of with considerable effort? What are some of the things you cling to that you can't imagine being able to let go of?

For this seven day period, spend one day focused on each of the seven factors of awakening: mindfulness, investigation, effort, joy, tranquility, concentration, and equanimity. Each day try to cultivate the factor of the day. To help you remember, write the factor down on a piece of paper and display it in a prominent place. Attempt small but frequent steps to make the factor more present, even at very mild levels. Are some factors easier for you to evoke than others? How does the increased presence of the factors affect you each day? What benefits come from working with the factors?

11

Eighth Factor: Right Concentration

When the Buddha knew that the householder's mind was ready, soft, free from hindrances, joyful and bright, he expounded the teaching special to the Buddhas.

—*(Middle Length Discourses 56.18)*

The final factor of the Eightfold Path is Right Concentration. The preceding seven factors all provide important support for our ability to develop a stable, focused, bright and concentrated mind. With the development of Right Concentration, the Eightfold Path can then culminate in insight and liberation.

Right Concentration prepares the mind for deep understanding and profound letting go. This occurs when the mind is "ready, soft, free from hindrances, joyful, and bright," as in the description above of the householder's mind, which the Buddha recognized as ready for the most significant teachings. Recognizing the expansive and unhindered quality of this mind is the task of the third foundation of mindfulness. Using this concentrated mind for wisdom is the task of the fourth foundation of mindfulness.

When we know how a concentrated mind is part of the Eightfold Path, we can use the possibility of the peaceful, expansive mind as a guidepost along the path. Rather than straining with striving and expectations, we cultivate receptive readiness. We let go deeply so that the mind can be free of tension. By understanding the value of a soft mind, we're less likely to get tense as we practice. When we remember the need to become free of the hindrances, we're less easily taken in by their authority. And when we understand the role of joy and mental brightness on the path, we will be quicker to recognize and support these states.

As befitting the metaphor of a journey along a path, the practice of Right Concentration itself involves a passage toward increasingly tranquil states of mind. In the same way that Right Mindfulness is a journey of deepening self-knowledge, Right Concentration moves us inward toward experiencing progressively deeper wellsprings of stillness and clarity.

With Right Concentration the mind becomes unified as it shifts from being scattered, disorganized, and agitated to becoming calm and centered. When agitated, the mind easily jumps between bodily sensations, emotions, moods, thoughts, daydreams, desires, external events, and our reactions to what we are experiencing. When concentrated, the mind settles down and stays centered and undistracted. As we relax into a focused attention there is a growing experience of unification, of feeling whole with all our faculties working in harmony.

The unification of mind that comes with concentration is reflected in the way the different factors that come into play with concentration all work together to support greater concentration. Relaxation and wholeness generate a feedback loop: concentration and unification relax the body, and the relaxed body supports further concentration; when concentration calms and brightens the mind, the calm and brightness sharpens concentration further; when concentration evokes joy or rapture, the joy provides incentive to further deepen the concentration and stillness.

Cultivating concentration takes patience and consistent practice. For most people concentration develops slowly, perhaps even imperceptibly with daily meditation practice. It can be useful to assume that only twenty-five percent of developing concentration is the intentional effort to stay present and focused; another twenty-five percent of the practice is an attitude of equanimity and receptivity; and a full fifty percent of concentration practice consists of letting go and relaxing.

All meditation practices develop concentration. Some practices have this as their primary purpose, while in other practices concentration is a by-product. One of the most common ways of developing concentration in meditation is to focus on breathing. Another approach is loving-kindness practice where one focuses on one of the three following aspects of the practice: the intentions of loving-kindness toward ourselves and others, the phrases repeated as part of the practice, or the feelings that arise while doing it. Still another way of developing concentrated, settled, undistracted mind can be focusing on the changing nature of present-moment experience, without emphasizing any particular object.

Concentration in meditation is not a laser-like focus originating in the "control tower" in the mind. Rather we cultivate it by physically and mentally settling our attention onto the object of focus with real intimacy. It requires letting go of distracting thoughts instead of forcibly pushing them away. To do this, it helps to calm whatever mental energy is involved in any thinking. Establishing a firm but soft intentness to stay focused is also helpful. Balancing this intentness with letting go into the object of concentration is useful.

It's best not to concentrate with brute mental force. Instead we can use our discernment to discover how to stay focused in a committed, relaxed way. We can develop wisdom about the hindrances to concentration and other forces that distract us. Instead of resorting to unhelpful tactics like aversion or resistance in the face of distractions, we can learn more effective strategies for overcoming them, leading to more tranquility and unification.

It is also useful to explore how to enjoy the practice. Not only can concentration practice bring joy, it can also bring tranquility and peace, sometimes to a greater degree than is usually available in daily life. Even small amounts of meditative joy and peace are useful for encouraging greater concentration.

A concentrated mind is a still mind, bright with awareness. As wonderful as this is, it is not an end in itself. Rather, for those walking the Eightfold Path, such a mind provides the clarity for deep insight and wisdom. In particular, deep concentration leads to penetrating insight into suffering and freedom from suffering. This in turn leads to a direct understanding of how true and useful the Four Noble Truths are.

The Four Noble Truths stand at the beginning and the end of the Eightfold Path. At the beginning they provide the orientation for Right View. At the end the Truths are affirmed by the insights Right Concentration makes possible. With greater wisdom into the Four Noble

Truths a person can then continue to walk the Eightfold Path with greater confidence and wisdom.

REFLECTIONS AND PRACTICES: RIGHT CONCENTRATION

Week 1 – The Conditions for Concentration in Daily Life

Recall a time in your life when you were especially concentrated in an enjoyable way. Was this episode associated with a period of your life, a particular activity, or a particular event? What external conditions fostered this concentration? What internal conditions within you supported this concentration? Which of the external and internal conditions did you have some choice over? Do you have some of this choice now? Is there a simple way that you could now recreate some of these conditions?

During this week put into place some of the conditions that support a more concentrated, calm, and alert mind. For example, you could focus on getting more sleep, exercise, free time, or relaxation. You could do more activities you enjoy or that nourish or renew you. Perhaps it helps to spend less time online or watching TV. After doing this for a week, evaluate the benefits of this exercise versus the effort it took to put these conditions in place. Were your efforts worth it?

Week 2 – The Experience of Concentration

Again this week, recall times when you have been concentrated, either recently or long ago. What did it feel like to be concentrated? What did it feel like to be focused, centered, or absorbed? What physical body sensations and feelings came with the concentration? What was your mind state at that time? Was calm or equanimity part of the experience? Were there any experiences of pleasure or enjoyment? What was your energy or vitality level like? Right after a period of concentration, how did you feel?

Focus on developing concentration in your meditation practice during this week. Make an effort to keep the mind on one object during the meditation period. If you are using the breath, you might count the breaths, from 1 to 10. If you lose count, simply start over at 1. As part of this emphasis on concentration, try to create conditions that support concentration. For example, do something relaxing or vitalizing just before you sit down to meditate. Consciously put aside concerns and preoccupations. As part of the concentration practice use any feelings, even preliminary feelings, of calm, stability, pleasure, enjoyment, or mental stillness as a kind of biofeedback to support further concentration.

Week 3 – Concentration and the Hindrances

Becoming skilled in concentration includes developing wisdom about the hindrances to concentration. The five hindrances of desire, ill will, sloth and torpor, restlessness and regret, and doubt are often listed as the primary obstacles to peaceful concentration emphasized in the Eightfold Path. Spend some time considering which of the five hindrances is most common for you. Spend time this week reflecting on how you can reduce the power and frequency of these hindrances in your meditation and in your life. Consider ways you can let go of your most common hindrances. Talk with a friend about your experiences of the hindrances.

Continue last week's practice of focusing on concentration during meditation. Notice which hindrances tend to be most common for you in this week's meditation. Stay alert so that you can let go of thoughts connected to the hindrances as soon as they occur. Just before sitting down to meditate spend some minutes considering how you can set aside or overcome the hindrances.

If you are unfamiliar with the five hindrances, you can read my articles on the hindrances which you can find on the Articles page of IMC's website (insightmeditationcenter.org). There is one article for each of the hindrances. For more information you can also read *Unhindered*, my book on the hindrances.

Week 4 – Concentration and Wisdom

The primary purpose of concentration is to facilitate deep insight and understanding. Spend some time reflecting on how being concentrated can help deepen understanding. In general, have you understood things better when you were concentrated and calm? How did the concentrated state contribute to your understanding? What can you learn from being concentrated that helps you become even more concentrated?

Over the course of this week focus your meditation practice on cultivating concentration. When you have become as concentrated as you think you will be during the meditation session, ask yourself what perspective on desire, aversion, clinging, thinking, and freedom you have from your current state of concentration. What does being concentrated teach you about the choices you can make in each present moment that lead to being caught or that lead to being free?

12

From the Eightfold Path to the Tenfold Path

For one who is concentrated, there is no need to intend:
"May I know and see things as they really are!"
It is a natural law for one with a concentrated mind
to know and see things as they really are.
—*The Buddha; Numerical Discourses 10.2*

The primary purpose of the Eightfold Path is to bring an end to greed, hate and delusion and the suffering that inevitably accompany them. In describing the fulfillment of this purpose the Buddha occasionally mentioned a Tenfold Path. In this expanded list, Right Knowledge and Right Release are added after the more familiar list of eight factors. The Eightfold Path creates the conditions for the ending of clinging and suffering; Right Knowledge is the insight that triggers Right Release, i.e., the cessation of suffering.

Right Knowledge is neither an abstract truth nor something we learn from a teaching; it isn't something mysterious or supernatural. As a continuation of the Eightfold Path, Right Knowledge is knowing firsthand the benefits experienced through living the path, and the suffering experienced when we don't live the path. The benefits include greater peace, compassion, well-being, integrity, and spiritual freedom. And the suffering includes all the familiar states we humans know so well—agitation, fear, conceit, greed, hostility, and more. The more fully we experience the benefits, the more clearly we see the differences between being attached and being free, having ill will and having goodwill, having ethical integrity and not having integrity. As we begin to make different choices, the contracted and agitated states of clinging begin to lose their appeal and their power over us, and we learn that they are neither hardwired nor necessary. As we see and experience healthy alternatives, these painful states begin to diminish in strength and frequency.

Right Knowledge is the understanding we gain from directly experiencing the absence of suffering. The more practicing the Eightfold Path alleviates suffering, the better we understand that clinging causes suffering. And experiencing the expansive, peaceful and happy states that come with the absence of clinging makes us increasingly sensitive to the reappearance of clinging, even in its most subtle forms. It becomes more and more clear that contracting, attacking, resisting and other expressions of greed, hate, and delusion are painful and cause harm.

Right Knowledge also includes recognizing that letting go of these contracted states and behaviors is reliable and trustworthy. It is not something we need to fear, even if what we are letting go of is our most precious and tenacious attachments to self. Freedom from clinging doesn't diminish us. Rather, it leads to some of the healthiest and most beneficial states of mind humans can experience.

Through the mindfulness and concentration factors of the Eightfold Path, Right Knowledge sees how all our perceptions and conceptions are in flux, constantly changing. With their fleeting appearance and disappearance they are not stable and thus cannot provide the fullest experience of peace. They cannot serve as the basis for a liberated mind. Instead, the basis for liberation is release.

Right Knowledge sets the stage for Right Release by helping the mind to relax and appreciate the process of letting go. Knowing the tangible suffering of clinging brings a disinclination to cling. Knowing the peace and well-being of non-clinging teaches that letting go of clinging is letting go into peace.

Right Release differs from ordinary letting go in that it has a bigger and more lasting impact. It is a ceasing of clinging so clear that Right Knowledge then becomes a knowing that is always available to us. In much the same way that we're no longer fooled by a magic trick once we've been shown how the trick is performed, a person who has experienced a mind released will begin to see through the tricks of the mind.

For most people Right Release is followed by a gradual process of becoming free in more and more areas of their life. The Buddha described these areas in terms of beliefs, biological drives, and subtle mental tendencies.

Because ultimate freedom does not, in itself, require any beliefs, Buddhism is particularly sensitive to the problems of clinging to beliefs, interpretations, and stories. An important part of living the Eightfold Path is loosening the grip on our views, including views about ourselves. A significant experience of release shows us that we don't need to be defined by any self-concept or identity.

More tenacious than clinging to beliefs is the clinging stemming from the drives of sensual desire and hostility. Even when people know that such clinging causes suffering it can be difficult to let go. Even the wisest people can easily succumb to these. This is where practicing the Eightfold Path is important. It provides a satisfying sense of well-being that is an effective alternative to desire or anger. Our strong drives can relax and fade away when something better is being experienced. Often enough, it is not helpful to be instructed to let go of desire and aversions. More useful is relaxing deeply, settling into a unified sense of being, and enjoying the pleasant feelings that can come with non-clinging. Sensual desire and hostility can then simply fade away.

The most difficult areas of clinging to overcome are subtle forms of conceit, agitation and ignorance. A person who is trying to let go of these can be caught in the conceit of individuality and personal agency. Sometimes the effort to let go agitates the mind. Believing there is something to let go of supports ignorance. The way to final release is to settle deeply into a relaxed, alert state where one doesn't try to do anything. Some people refer to this as a state of equanimity. Others refer to it as resting in being. It is with this kind of ease that the mind can let go of itself.

The Eightfold Path is called a noble path because of the integrity and dignity it bestows. As it is not dependent on beliefs, those who walk this path do not champion Buddhism in opposition to the beliefs of others. In overcoming clinging, people on the path do not create conflict. Instead, practicing the Eightfold Path develops an open mind, an open heart, and an open hand. May this openness be of benefit to the whole world.

Ven Ananda said to the Buddha:
"Venerable sir, this is half of the holy life, that is, good friendship, good companionship, good comradeship."

The Buddha answered:
"Not so, Ananda! Not so, Ananda! This is the entire holy life, Ananda, that is, good friendship, good companionship, good comradeship. When practicioners have a good friend, a good companion, a good comrade, it is to be expected that they will develop and cultivate the Noble Eightfold Path.

Acknowledgements & Gratitude

It is with much gratitude and appreciation that I acknowledge everyone who helped with this book. Diana Clark, Ines Freedman, Shelley Gault, Carol Ghiglieri, and Kathi Olsen provided great editing support. Elena Silverman was masterful in designing and laying out the book for printing. Evan Winslow Smith, using his original photograph, designed the cover.

Most of the chapters in this book began as talks given to practitioners at the Insight Meditation Center. Without an audience eager to learn about the Eightfold Path this book would not exist. Not only am I grateful to those who listen to my teachings, I am inspired by the sincere interest and dedicated practice of many, many people. It is an inspiration that fuels my own practice and encourages me to continue to learn how to live the Eightfold Path.

ABOUT THE AUTHOR

Gil Fronsdal is the founding teacher at the Insight Meditation Center in Redwood City, California and at the Insight Retreat Center in Santa Cruz, California. He has been engaged in the practice, study, and teaching of Buddhism for over forty years, having started practicing when he was twenty.

Gil has an extensive collection of Dharma talks on a wide range of topics related to mindfulness and Buddhist practice. They can be accessed at Audiodharma.org.

Gil spent time as Buddhist monk in monasteries in the US, Japan, Thailand, and Burma. He has a Ph.D in Buddhist Studies. As a Dharma teacher he has written *The Issue at Hand*, *Unhindered*, and *The Monastery Within*. As a translator he has translated *The Dhammapada* and, under the title of *The Buddha Before Buddhism*, an ancient collection of verses called the *Atthakavagga*. As a scholar he has written *Dawn of the Bodhisattva Path: The Early Perfection of Wisdom*, a study on the origins of Mahayana Buddhism.

The gift of Dharma surpasses all gifts.
The taste of Dharma surpasses all tastes.
The delight of Dharma surpasses all delights.
The destruction of craving conquers all suffering.
                    —*The Buddha (Dhammapada, verse 354)*